The Taxidermist's Cut

The Taxidermist's Cut

Rajiv Mohabir

Four Way Books
Tribeca

Please direct all inquiries to:
Editorial Office
Four Way Books
POB 535, Village Station
New York, NY 10014
www.fourwaybooks.com

Library of Congress Cataloging-in-Publication Data

Mohabir, Rajiv.
The taxidermist's cut / Rajiv Mohabir.
pages ; cm
ISBN 978-1-935536-72-7 (softcover : acid-free paper)
I. Title.
PS3613.O376A6 2016
811'.6--dc23

2015028577

This book is manufactured in the United States of America and printed on acid-free paper.

Funding for this book was provided in part by a generous donation in memory of John J. Wilson.

Four Way Books is a not-for-profit literary press. We are grateful for the assistance
we receive from individual donors, public arts agencies, and private foundations.

[clmp]

We are a proud member of the Community of Literary Magazines and Presses.

Distributed by University Press of New England
One Court Street, Lebanon, NH 03766

For Anjani Devi Prashad

Contents

PREFACE

Let's pretend you are going hunting.
You pack a buck knife, a bow,
arrows cleft from straight weeds, wild
in my front yard. You perch in an oak,
yearning for the chill that signals
harvest. The copper of pine needles falls;
whether you catch me or not is not the point.
You look first at wandering deer, the bigger prize,
full of meat, with hide to cure, but keep an eye
peeled for upland birds too, smaller,
easier to mount once ensnared. You don't need
a guide to hollow lungs of song. *Yes,* I said,
birds are easy to work with, refugee bones
that gift flight, delicate and slight,
may as well be shadow. I have always
made myself invisible. I mean to say
I am still—this trembling breath of a comma,
this coincidental object of your want.

3

Rural Sports (erasure poem)

In glade nets, stretched across narrows,
riding from tree to tree, for night-flying
woodcocks or wild ducks lay a trap
on the ground. Nets of fine black silk
slack, the bird, taken with certainty,
attempts to pass as whole. I recall seeing
two men: one man was let down,
the other, looked after the safety
of the manrope, gripping his iron bar.
I have been between heaven and earth
once or twice, dared the edge lying
upon my breast. The faintest battle
between land and sea—

below guillemots flying off in droves,
little black specks in white foam.

ORTOLAN

Take the bird alive and blind it.
Keep it in a windowless room,

or if there are windows, board them up.
It's important that no light gets in

and that the bunting cannot dream its body.
Feed this creature of god figs, millet,

grapes so it gorges and engorges,
unrecognizable. Drown the Ortolan

in Armagnac, snuff out the light
in a snifter, so its belly and lungs fill

with liqueur of the hereafter. When you
put this songbird between your lips

and bite down, veil your face
with my mother's silk sari.

Hide your gluttony from the god
with hungry dog-eyes who envies

our nocturnal commotion. Taste the burst
of liqueur-flowers from the lungs

on your tongue. Taste the entire life
in the dark. Taste every man

who has ever put me in his mouth.

COVER SCENT

He lies naked with another boy in a clearing
of palmettos and sand pines.

They touch each other
with rabbit skin gloves.

Today: the odium of salt and pheromones.
To erase himself he rubs the ashes

on his arms and chest. Outside an
Eastern Cottontail hides three kits.

*

The steel jaws ensnare the mother,
the other boy runs to the dark river to bathe.

He picks up a kit and strokes it,
drawn from the den, it's silk on his palm.

This is not he with rust-oil smears under
his fingernails—

what he draws he draws in ash.

The Complete Tracker

Bent-kneed, interpreting signs
      I trek the wreckage of myths:
toadstools on a felled tree, or

the crescent-shaped impression
      from a hart's escape to his denning
ground. His hoof print is a split heart.

As a phantasm you wander
      a remote path. Lost, I open
the guidebook, its spine rolls.

It reads, *Examine closely the leaf-strewn*
      forest floor on the way to low-
lying shorelines. Every creature

that moves on earth leaves
      a mark of its passing,
though the trails are seldom linear.

I may never find my way back—
      Your prints canter northward
where in a blue jumper and wild hair you said,

After the rut, bucks lose interest.
      Trailing anyone proves a gamble on wet clay.
You folded your route scribbled on

a diner's placemat and left.
Now your voice is placeless,
a coyote howl in velvet.

Your footprints are covered over
by leaves and other men's heavy soles.

CANIS LATRANS

"The colonized then tend to break into song."
—Franz Fanon from *The Wretched of the Earth*

Do not mistake yourself
for a wolf, your plantation days
        of illiterate indenture still

dusk the horizon. Crouch in the field
        of yellowing cane, your ears
and snout obscure your form, your skin

        sings one song while people hear
another. Your grandmother picks
        a book from the shelf and folds

it into her bag. She takes it to market
        to wrap the fish she buys. You descend
from a misread line of poetry

        that grasped a cutlass.
You cannot change your hide—
        your parents are not from India

and only curse in Bhojpuri.
        Other Indians don't know
your drawl, and laugh

at your rustic coat. You split from them
for Skeldon and Lusignan. Here,
        everyone calls your camouflage a different name—

some *jackal, brush wolf,* some *shudra,* or *sand
        nigger.* Americans fear you
will kidnap their litter, drag them

        from jump ropes, jaws locked around
blonde heads. They misread poverty
        for poetry. At dusk, cry these spirits

        into old Hindi film songs.
They will clink as ice
        in your glass of rum.

TRIP LINE

In the morning I say, *I don't care*
if the broken line is my fault.

A friend warns me to touch nothing
when examining a trail to avoid leaving my scent.

I say, *I have disturbed as much as I could,*
walked over a mile and never picked up my feet—

The trick is to gather enough bedclothes
to predict a lover's comings and goings

with fair precision. In the dark, string a thread
across the trail that leads from the bed to the road.

Wedge the thread under a piece of bark
or a split twig on the corner of the road,

and tie the other end to the bedpost.
When he strays the chord will snap.

A buck in velvet, I once saw a stag fooled
by a hunter's call. I still trip on the clear voice

of the first man who scraped off my soft casing.
I cannot tell from the upturned sand

and drying oak leaves, is my own tibia,
my crown, my own buckling antler broken?

Is the thread snapped by my reoccurring dream
where I string one end to you,

the other to my hatchback and drive off,
flooring the damn thing?

Ritual

You're a pro at peripheral. Years after
you are cities apart,

you meet up your first boyfriend
for coffee and gin. He convinces you

to park in the Methodists' lot,
to undo your jeans. You spit out

teenage sacrament on the pavement. Watch
the lips close. Repeat. Repeat.

It goes like this:
you will hate yourself until

you push your arms through
your orange long-sleeve

and withdraw the marble box
from the dark. Inside is a sword.

Inside is a mantra that calls
blood to the skin

you never asked for. Repeat.
Repeat. Watch

it cover over, the lips of your arm
closing. Repeat.

In the bar you drown
in scotch haze;

the man opposite you will blaze
in your throat when his denim

and leather are a nest
calling birds to their weaving

from the pile on your floorboards.
You no longer cut as a child cuts.

It's morning and you swallow
the sun's fever but not its light.

Outside your brother's pastor rains brimstone:
your tongue will rot

in your mouth; flames
will crack your bones into Psalms.

It's Christmas. It's polarity:
a chasm within

so large you don't remember
what's divided.

The Taxidermist's Cut

In the taxidermist's tool belt:
      pinking irons
      hand vise
      knife
      Bondo
      fleshing beam
      skinning table
      razor

From *Practical Taxidermy*:
"And the learner having got out the whole of the knives and whetstone may proceed."

Your great grandparents traveled kalapani from India to South America. It tries to erase you still, though you cannot hide brown skin and burnt cumin in Chuluota, where active members of the Klan rally against sand niggers and faggots. The name Econlockhatchee means "River of Mounds" in Seminole which may mean "runaway" in Spanish. Florida's black water flows northward.

When you come here, you come to be outside of brown and unbrown.

On the banks of the river, the wet sand keeps a record of all who pass. Walking south against the flow, away from the St. Johns River stamps of *canid* footprints trail yours.

You are being stalked.

Canis latrans are new to Florida. Their needs in habitat and diet are nonspecific and there is reduced competition in the scrubland. They adapt easily, experts at elusion. Their pelts hang by the dozens at the Sanford Flea Market—hated for being exotic, invasive, and competition for jobs.

Most white folks see coyotes as wolves.

But you are not from the subcontinent and you don't descend from first-wave doctors and lawyers, but from illiterate farmers who were once slaves in the sugarcane fields for the East India Company. Your own country cannot be here. You limn night.

Erasure

Dress the animal in the field.

With your hands reach
                into the thoracic cavity
and pull
            the intestines,
                        stomach,
        liver,
the kidneys,
                    lungs.

            Blood will stain the grass.

                Leave entrails
                        for crows.
                Lay the coyote
                        on the skinning table.
                Cut from the anus
                        to the top of his shoulders.
                Look into his eyes—

You can take a Christian name to blend in at the First Baptist Church, though they may still kick you out—the coyote in the henhouse—for the dreams they have of people like you.

The youth leader looks at your summer coat and laughs, *I wouldn't see you but your eyes are so big and your teeth are so white.* At night they see your teeth grinning *a Satanic grin.* Watch the elders magnify the Lord.

Every time you speak they hear a different hell.

Along the house's stucco, the exoskeletons cling, cut through in a single slice. An echo without being seen. All about, air clouds with cicada song. You have never seen one up close, still invisible.

Their wings a web of veins leading into music. Their eyes are so large they can bury themselves in earth for seventeen years, know instinctually when the threat is a memory. Their wings are harps. Place the shell in your palm.

A queer flutter knocks about your ribs.

Erasure

Make an incision at the front leg
just below the footpad—

                        cut up to the elbow
along where fur
changes from tawny
                to white.
         This is a natural line to follow.

When the meat is exposed
cut the hide away
                from the muscle
      in all four legs.

                Then connect the foreleg
                knife trail to the shoulder cut.

                    In this way you have removed the skin,
                        separating it from the legs.

                You may start on the back—
            Do with the tail
                as you did with the feet.

All points lead back to the anus.

From *Home Taxidermy for Pleasure & Profit:*
"The learner is apt to come to grief."

You spend your life eating darkness. With the first cut across the pubis and lower belly a murder of crows lifts into clouds on purple feathers—

Leave a slug trail of spit beetle-nut red. Chew. Spit blood on the sidewalk. You always want to refashion yourself into some other self.

You always wanted a pair of your own bangles. These musical instruments are Creole teeth marked with flowers. You want to pull out all of your teeth.

With gold forceps forged from your mother's bangles you extract the map of India. Or its shadow.

With a razor, cut   against the commandments of

                                            every book.

Remember not to cut
             through more skin
than is necessary,
as you will have to sew

up the holes you make
             along the way—

Remember kneeling before the white man with the plastic scrotum hanging from his pickup. He didn't say *when* and laughed. But before you slip his underwear around his ankles you must prove loyalty to him, then to the U.S. First, you must swallow a minnow whole then jump from the bridge on Snow Hill Road. When you finish, you must swear never to eat curry and daal with your fingers.

Take off your skin right here. Dress yourself for the field. Pull out your entrails and stuff your yellow belly with coals.

Pick up the razor.

It sounds like *erasure*.

Dress for the first time you cut yourself. Blood erupts. New flesh to grow between these banks of skin. A river first.

Then young earth without a secret.

It's raining outside.

Your parents are at Bible study, leaving you alone with the devil inside. Your clothes are strewn about the floor.

The rain ricochets drops through the windowpane.

Your drops drone and soar from the opened window as cicadas.

Inside you rain. You are a forgery. Not a wolf. Not an Indian. Not a son.

The first time you drag that razor down your wrist and forearm, the rubies grow veined wings, tymbals. Large eyes push through the cut.

Despite the dark pools collecting at the edges of the table, despite the darkness of suffocation, a steady flutter. Cut along the large intestine, through the diaphragm and along the ribcage. It cracks as it opens.

—*splay the hide when the flesh
is removed. Wash the blood*

and cholesterol into the river.

Take the brown skin with the coat intact; it can erase you easily though it too is brown. Its brown changes, from yellow-grey, to red, to tawny. Against the dawn, who can make out the clear outline of the forest?

Cover your own skin with the hide that does not hide. Place your arms and legs in the empty pelt and sew yourself up.

Before running into the woods catch a dusk-calling or lyric cicada. You released them decades ago and now they cling to sentinel oak bark. Keep caged in your closed teeth its flitting, though it tickle your tongue. Against the sun falling or rising it will drone and hum and buzz.

On the forest line a coyote's silhouette sings a cicada song.

∫∫∫

TEAR

This is a delicate operation.
To reduce tears: allow the body
to thaw. Wet the bird's down

in a rainbow of melted snow,
black ice, asphalt, oils softening
until he is a starry night. Until

he overdoses from ecstasy.
Until eyes secrete a dark fluid
when punctured. I dream

I am bent over, gripping our radiator,
impaled. A starling pliés
from my dark pool. With a pirouette,

he flutters, beats his beak
against the skylight glass. Pierce
his eye so he snags his skin

on the window latch, skittish
from dazzling white. Sparking,
he lights on the ledge to gaze

into the haze graying dawn
and shakes stars from
his feathers—

Watch his diamonds twinkle
as they strike tile.

Bondo

You reach in the medicine cabinet
and fumble past quartered cardstock,
polyester resins, spliced articles, lavender
flowers crushed, their oils extracted, for
a jar of Sulfur moths you caught in your
childhood. Then, they tickled your palms,
as you learned a lover's tongue would, or a
lover's ghost. The fluorescent lights shiver
a cold silence and you hear wings beat out
seconds—

The mirror says you are dark holes
of inversed projections wreathed in
Lepidoptera wings, scales for masking
the habit of covering up the *wires after
you attach a mount to a drift wood base,*
piercing its Jesus side with a pushpin to
craft an eternal display. What do you cast
in its hollow after excavating its thorax?
Will you make new myths of Bondo, your
fingertips brown with a wing's powder?

You smash the jar, the moths pierced by
glass shards, flutter at first, windup birds
flop on a razor sea into stillness.

AT THE WINDOW

For flaming wings there is no choice. I enter the darkened house. A need that breaks glass and scars stories across my forearm. Your reflection glints across the pane. I enter an empty room. A hollowed bed and sunshine in squares.

[*a rapping at the window*]

My thumb was cut quick and your lips reddened from playing flute. You skitter. In the mirror behind the clock you flutter and I want to be back inside you.

[*a rapping*]

Our shadows are still flitting in the hallways. That night I chipped my tooth on your belt buckle, you shook violently into dust, your song drying down your throat. I sat so still until I began to disappear. First my arms—

[*frenzied tapping at the glass*]

I walk to wash you from my hands. On the window ledge, a slight heap—a cardinal's hollow body, crushed by the force of hurling itself into its own reflection.

ORACLE

In the garden you keep a buck skull on a pole. *It keeps holes from the squash,* you say. The slight beak marks are prognostications. You shuffle a deck and draw the Five of Cups—what remains goes unnoticed. Once we drove through the snow in January and you found a Yellow-throated Vireo on the oak porch with a frosted rostrum but still forecasting the future. You squeezed your palms together. Blue songbird arteries erupted from beneath rust and canary feathers. I touched the floor with my whiskey nose that night. You held my arms behind me. You pulled endless scrolls from my ribs—a ghazal repeating *we are never owned.* You write your name in your fingerprints along my back and swear them a holy scrawl.

FIELD CARE

To preserve the memory you wait
        amongst reeds twisting
   a decoy call. Your shadow induces
         pulse to frenzy; the game bird flies.

       You shoot once. It thrashes
   on the grass as you approach
     in boots and break its wings
with one word from your lips, *Come.*

       With you, Sajana, I have no peace.

I writhed to your will that day:
      when James grabbed my hand;
   what else can you prize after the punch
      to my throat or my spitting blood for days?

      If a pheasant is shot hard, its carcass
 will never appear to fly after death.
    And now, what good is this shell
of skin, my chest emptied quickly

      in the field of sheets with clumsy blade strokes:
    a harvest of flesh and fluid
 wreaking damage to my breast feathers?
   No matter how well you prepare

this memory, doctored to reshape
                my chest against your back,
                      I am not inside that skin you fix.

PRESERVATION (ERASURE POEM)

Procure the amateur's toughness.
                    Seize the bird by the sides,

insert poisons and other pain,
                    a wine bottle full of spirits,

and rub well the skin.
                    I remember seeing a stuffed cock: an effigy

that perfectly satisfied.
                    The bone close to the body shines

whitely in front of you, though
                    insects may devour this casing.

GANGA

I do not know leatherwork,
the back break of cane;

I never whetted Grandfather's
cutlass nor kirpan,

never uddered cows, churned
milk into yogurt to soothe—

my back never rose rubies from
lash tracks tracing ship routes back

around that cragged Cape where
Good Hope failed us.

My navel could never berth
Vishnu's lotus,

could not crack the skulls
of our incinerating dead,

guide Grandmother's soul
into her new body.

CORENTYNE

What a soul remembers:

My face sticky with Berbice—
stolen mangoes from papa's neighbor,

a home held together
with hay, mud, bottom-house—

the first time I saw the Milky Way
break speckles on the river's face.

Gleaming back-dam sun jewels:
brilliant singsong star-lilt,

Akash-Ganga constellations on dark skin.

This body of earth, star, pitch, straw,
house of continents.

THAMES

Go home Paki

My Fair Lady spit on my mother,
split her eyebrow into a trickling silk

pink slick shone on pavement gray. She lay
pooling a sari plait in queen's country.

Go home Paki

She could not pleat cemented blood
into a sari nor recall what had dried

to flow in her veins. How could she exhume
a riverbed of parched Bhojpuri bones—

Go home Paki

English National Front and Ma tucked me
in her Creole cotton.

Paki go home

I am from queen's country,
show me the way *home.*

ECONLOCKHATCHEE

Tannin browned Seminole stream,
I bathed in this river.

A pot—wholly of this clay,
filled heavy with feral tea.

At fourteen I learned the truth.
Whelps dog into rebel flags,
tree coons, hunt fags.

I did not play inside his house,
but drank from his outside hose,

more than once he gripped
my pine. More than once,

he jammed me, in Southern Baptist
conviction, into steel lockers.

> *Brown fairy bitch, go*
> *back where you came from.*

He followed me home that night
bat in tow, my skull still

in one Chuluota piece.

HUDSON

Kettledrum barrage, I beat tassa
down Broadway, in hymn,

in rain, a ghost ship *him*.
Her Majesty's forgotten

son never sets on haldi fingers,
on chutney lips, never sets on Liberty

Avenue bangle clink. A song,
home spun into sinew, into five

generations gone. SS Jura's board-
grooves curl the kalapani strain

onto mast of muscle, of bone;
woven into patchwork sails, smooth,

I am sailing. Now, I am sailing.

Once you swallowed a man
and the earth followed. A placenta

of knotted clots and krill poured out
in a birthing ceremony. This skin is a sieve.

Once a man jumped into coral, rode
your dorsal into darkness. You held the sun

pelagic in your chest to chart
the gouges across the abyss burning

in your own gold. You dove
into silence you could not break,

gripping wonder between your lattice of daggers,
until the sun dusked and you sank

beneath the sheet of horizon.
There is joy in night. It summons you

between continents to whisper
prayers into its ink. Once a fisherman took off his face;

mistook himself for shadow; and plunged
his hook into your new moon night

to implant his false god of fear
into your liver until you surfaced

gasping, *Let there be light.*
And what flared from you, scattering

as a herring shoal, that shot in beams
from your skin as you took his hand

and kissed it? Now every
voyager looks over the bow

to see you. What darkness endures
if this body is a lantern?

WEST INDIAN MANATEE

You don't belong in freshwater, yet here you walk
the streets humming Mohammad Rafi, *Don't leave,*

my heart is not yet filled. A queer sight
in the Homosassa River. Make yourself minuscule.

The drab river fish gossip about your brown skin
throughout Chuluota though your daddy dances

like a jackal for the man with a Bible-page tongue,
recites The Pledge to erase his accent.

The police still stop you, check your head for rags.
They want to brew a potion of your bones,

to shake off the sand from the Star Spangled Banner.
Peel off your shirt. Show the white scars

along your arms to the sunshine. Hold
your breath and disappear into a limestone cavern

before their boats' propellers begin to whir.

MALLOTUS VILLOSUS

Yearly, capelins throw themselves
onto the beach in silver sparkles,

gifting flesh to eagles and
rapacious gulls stalking foam.

They flock to flip and flail of writhing bodies
trying to swim while beached. Skilled at navigating

away from harm, away from squid beaks,
mackerel, seal and beluga teeth, they hurl

themselves into the danger of drowning in sky,
to slake this biology of desire, braving waves

that bash them cold against pulverized shells.
Blood drives them to synchronize with tide—

far from home yet drying in it. The challenge here
is to survive the tide of those who would devour.

I have drowned in need, in warmth of breath,
in another's pulse, content to risk annihilation

whether by sun, whether by muscle tearing talons
able to crack the cage of my chest, or to surrender

to madness beyond control of this single sheath.

∫∫∫

[Last Night] in Jackson Heights [This Morning] With Him, Not You

[That day you had your birth-chart drawn up by Pallavi]

The Venusian mound of your palmate palm's
meat, meatier than mine or
        mound of Saturn flesh,
                            you are one whole
return ahead, falling body
onto sheet from street
        or that Indian-hot means
                              Jai-Kisan Heights and

you will not speak (to me) for two days.

[Last night]

It's hardly an April forecast and you still hold back,
have not invited me inside.
                                    Inside that library of the broken
                you keep record of every fallen star(fish)
you skipped. On 74th street where a golden record
plays in traffic (before the store).

(Shamshad Begum to Lata Mangeshkar: both standing up):
        What joy is there in drinking tears,
        what you keep inside will stifle—

[With him]

What is there to fear—

Midnight samosas with him, where green
chutney burns deep after
                              I lick his lips.

[With Him]

The speakers in the roti shop croon
               the Babla and Kanchan tunes and
he is more Lahore than my GT
                      and Berbice-Creek;
       Urdu in waves of Karachi,   my own chutney
         of Creole and Hindi—

broken like the mast   of a ship   that sails
         the Caribbean to Asian Sea. Him fair
     wind and me kalapani—
                  black waters.

What do the tides erase between us
               on Liberty Avenue in Queens,
    my should-be home, the A train shadows
of salara,   phulowri,   katahar,
                 and curry?

Desi aureola enveloping us whole, a ship
          from this world   to the next
           what does it matter
I am the dark areola and he the skin
           as we lie, him on me, pressed
breast to lip
   and lip to chest?

[This morning]

Cast as a map,
       in the Nastaliq
of his curling black
       hair, a curving qawwali

across his Punjabi chest.

[Last night]

He says, *Mughal-e-Azam was the first film*
 hand-painted into Technicolor—

the highest grossing until Sholay in 1975,
 the homoerotic classic.

(I say, *The flames keep their own colors.*)

Across from Famous Pizza, in the Palika Bazaar
 of Jackson Heights,

you ask me if I consider myself white.
 I imagine dipping a brush into the fallen

stars in my own hands to paint you Technicolor.

[Yesterday during the day]

Playback singers play back on the streets in Queens, back
       to front in the street named Kalpana Chawla
Way after the first astronaut of Indian

       descent in space, a fallen (Punjabi) star. A suitcase-
sized gash blasted the side, allowed the hot space gasses in. You almost
       held your Jupiter-recessed palm

to mine when you spoke. What of the joy of now—
       the problem is I can't wait for your Venus-promise
to chase me shooting-star straight across Asia.

One day, remembering this, we will smile and see—
haan ji, we will see.

Carolina Wren

A child sketches an echo from the skittish
        bird, hollowed and filled with cotton
behind glass at the Museum of Natural History. He asks
        his mother, *How did this one die?*

On my mother's porch, a mother
        wren nested amongst Rhododendron roots.
Her eggs hatched into naked skins. I read,
        Wrens reject their young if a boy should touch,

or be touched by, another boy but only after
        I wrapped it in my fingers. Beginning
to fledge, mother smelled only a child's
        foreign oils. She abandoned the touched chick.

I flew north to the branch of the live oak,
        singing rust of the forest hammock.
Outside glass doors a songbird washes
        his feathers of any scent in the melting snow.

Inside, half the exhibit is closed.
        How will this child survive being cast out
or abandoned for what he cannot change?

Consider the Painted Bunting on the porch,
the most beautiful bird in North America,

named for Scylla who betrayed her father
for her lover's sake.

He left Crete by ship. Her father, disgusted
by her perfidy, transformed her into the Keiris bird.

All night I cast my plume after Cretan ships
into the Aegean throb,

flapping against the brine, after a man's vessel.
An eagle paints surf in shadow.

Dear Father, forgive me
for what your body made me,

for what I perverted, being a man
and taking another.

When he lays bare-chested in my nest
of down and vespertine, which betrayal

can a son endure: *a father's beating*
with wings, or his own body?

CUTTER

You are a falconer without a glove;
      a raptor barebacks your ulna.
Every scar along your wrist
      is a lifeline lifting to flight. A father's

hand span around your throat
      chrysalises into butterfly wings.
The truth is you'd rather be
      ash. You expunge sin, prophesy:

one day a man will kiss you
      from palm to elbow. Now,
hide your darkness in lines—
      who reads poetry anyway?

When you cut mouths along your forearm
      your whole body gasps.

Raised by Crows

I

Koyals thrust eggs from crows' nests.
Albumens and yolk puddle on the
ground. Owned by surrogates, the
fledgling cannot reflect in any standing
water, pushed from twigs and string,
woven into a new web of difference.

II

I arrive in New York in fall, searching
for my face in East Village windows,
wielding an adulterous English, saying
neemakharam for *infanticide*. Instead
of *to bite back the East India Company's
salting hand,* I say *slavery.* This matted
world's silks and fast food feathers me
into a beast a mother can't know. She
asks, *Why is the child's body so dark yet
speaks like a ghost?*

III

In this Creole city, they call us *coolie.* I
return to Libery Avenue in the summer,
singing: *O jhulo jhulo kanhai palana.* I buy
jamun and sapadilla with the speckled
skin of the *anya-vapa,* that koyal raised

by crows, nurtured on half-digested
vocabulary placed onto his tongue by
Her Majesty's sugar lust.

"... every culture is first and foremost national."
—*The Wretched of the Earth,* Franz Fanon

Once an India-man in Florida said,
Guyanese aren't real *Indians.*
You stand before a mirror,

what glass won't distort
        your image? Even the eye's lens
twists coyotes into wolves

        one hundred twenty-five years
outside of the desh. Orientalists
        well documented the gray wolf

for associations with affluence.
        Do you expect others to see
nuance speckling your pelt when

        your coolie mother can't tell
Gujarati from Punjabi? Put on
        your janitor coat and some

think you a doctor. Coming
        to the States, your own parents
didn't have the right papers, caste,

or ship passes. You are a coyote
in wolf's clothes. Your father warns,
      Desis will reject you; the temple

pack will extirpate the untouchable.
      To them West Indian means
palaces, rubies, samosas; to your

Chuluota pelt it's Aji's gold
      teeth, kitchen Creole, two spoons
of ice cream in your sweet rice.

To A Father Who Can't Accept His Son

Weren't you ever helpless? Listen,
at twelve I shot down

a blackbird from the tree;
you praised me
          for my eye,
It's what all boys do.
In a flash of purple—

              black—
              blue—

I dyed my robes in the cis-
tern of patriliny.
          Remember
yourself as a fledgling,
naïve, reaching out
          for any hand?

If my story angers you
I am not sorry.
          I regretted my fall.

Will you uproot
          all of the trees where I hid
the animal until it lifted
to the branches?

Will you burn my poems?

After dinner I cupped
　　　the black fruit of the Tree
　　　of Knowledge
　　　　　　　of Violence:

where welts rose on my legs
from the riding crop hidden
by your headboard,
　　　　　　　the crumble of song
shuddered in my hands.

URSUS THIBETANUS

An Asian black bear dances,
gray fur wreathing his eyes, his dress
smeared in blood's rust.
Chained, his paws tear at iron cuffs.

He dances to the Madari's count, who recites
a child's book of prayers in verse:
as punishment for once stealing an apple,
the Madari keeps the bear far

from the sight of other bears,
away from the spring of pine;
in summer, away from glacial streams.
My father's favorites are verses of a god

he keeps in a pristine book, unopened
on the highest shelf. It demands that the son
lay down as a ram on a table of stone;
a sacrificial blade to slit his throat

into an eternal smile. When I was young,
in my father's den, I opened his highest volume
and snapped its spine. In pencil I wrote:
apples grow from arsenic filled seeds;

bears in the wild are omnivorous, frightened
by the cadence of prayer. And from
my lips, I cast off these chains of *amen.*

The Right Tool for the Job

I replace each
beautiful simul
accustomed to
your every me
refused me at y
now I lay arms

feather with your
acra. You grow
latex. It spills into
mory: that day you
our bare back. And
—instruments to

invade me for
my knees to my
and my organs
blood and fiber.
and your palm,

the sounds I make,
neck. Your fingers
shift, a bomb of
Between my heart
only a thin layer.

/REN/人

Cactus wren amasses fur, paper, cotton into a needle-crowned nest—her eggs.

This hole deadens saguaro from chest down, a deadened pair of legs
      dangle below a hollowed chunk drying in Mojave air

—or sometimes her song is her only sighting.

Wrens love one another lifelong: brown stripes, breathing fire-songs, or—

Sometimes saguaro flowers bloom late afternoon. Saving what a wren-body
      remembers of plenty, it spends round calcium, a reason for home—

—or sun or desert winds scorch broken eggs and home into ash or broken
      cacti.

Saguaro stands its highest, feels for as long as the nest endures eggs or other
      shoots of other saguaros.

You burrowed into my chest.

We loved each other once into Pentecostal tongues and blood or the diverging
      line in Mandarin for human heartedness pronounced /ren/.

Wren nests in any convenient home.

You feathered me into dummy home; the day you left I burned standing.

Paynes Prairie, Gainesville

Puddles pock the prairie. A buffalo trail
and a whole forest are lost

to limestone fall, a shallow
water table, and a homophone for pain.

Once I played flute to your guitar
and the sun rose then thorned. You sang

beneath the signs warning *Danger Bison*—
our songs themselves ghosts.

I admit failure to a friend:
I have never spelled *love* with another

in the tangle of my own limbs.
She says, *If you can't prove it empirically,*

it doesn't exist, and asks, *What is it*
about naming things—

I repeat to myself, *Danger Bison*
and lie to myself through our mythology.

We heard buffalo roam the prairie yet
we find a barred owl's flight feathers—

the echo of a night stalker, streaked
brown on white.

Reference and Anatomy

Outside of our home a baby sparrow is crushed into cement,
wings outstretched, beak parted slightly.
Hollow radius and ulna erupt through gashes
in skin. Many dreams I don't tell you.
Winter blankets us again; I ask, *What is the relationship*
between my ear canals and mouth?
The secret: I already know how to ply
the whole carcass as a death mask. I tell you,
You must first understand a human's inclinations—
your nail beds are filled with fresh soil, hair ripped
out by the roots, and semen. Noticing the details
of your smaller areas, I ask, *Whose semen is it?*
This is a roadmap to a life-like mount, you say,
I am mapping where the hollow goes.
There are many men's fingerprints up
and down my own thighs. You ask me their names
so you can stuff them inside me. I smile, *They're all there,*
frozen in thick sheets of lake ice, corpses
gossiping about exactly where and for how long
I've tongued each man—
You pluck nimbus feathers, to search for
the underlying structure as you position me—
You say anything I say to you is a fairytale.

∫∫∫

Taxidermy for Pleasure

Along the cornfield's edge, my nose
held high in the breeze, I recast you flitting back
to the skyline between your male redolence

and the salt of morning's approach.
Today you are words in the paper,
If you start fixing things, the replication will consume you—

There is no today, only yesterday's atrophy
where I fix you in palmetto scrub. You were the first
to call to me in this quail's flat, then rising pitch,

and we were the last pair in the covey.
Yes, on the edge of that dove field I sky-burst
with other boys. I drank that whir of wing there

by the over grown clump of honeysuckle with you,
under chain link in hidden acreage,
unwilling to molt down for flight—

You turned to me every evening until one
when the roaring guns in the backwoods and the canter
of spooring retrievers caught us.

Homosexual Interracial Dating in the South in Two Voices (erasure poem)

Do not mix your orders of birds
ignoring their enemies from different
parts of the world. I have seen
one or two in "Black Country."
A scarlet ibis mounted in a case
on china gasolier, need I warn
against such flights of art? I might
advise upon the subject: keep straight
like two arrows or sticks.

                                      Nature must fail.
The amateur may fall, being artistic
and natural. I never saw progress
unless a couple of young foxes
in front of their earth, in a declaration
of love, tumble at the water-jump,
riding to win, scramble after their
steeds.

You dirty boy.

                                      Judgment in full-
cry might be executed by men seeing
this sort of thing and laughing at
the injurious epithets applied to my
perturbed spirit. These people know
little.

ANOLIS CAROLINENSIS

On the trampoline's mesh
I crucified the emerald shift of bodies.
If the anole's tail didn't snake off

in muddy legged pursuit I'd pierce
it too, burning to shed my dark. I'd escape
setting a trail of rubies slithering

into palmettos, leaving to discover
masturbation with my neighbor.
Telling the truth in Limacol baptism rituals

lifted from the LBW, I was Jesus
in the garden, wanting to be rid of this cup,
this tail, this false god.

Maybe detached from myself
the god of butterflies would change
my colors so Southern boys

wouldn't see my palms stay soft.
I have never claimed to be brave.

TIBICEN AULETES

Your dread deafens you. Your body
will not stop humming odd secrets.

Last night you spent sweat with the guy
you Grindr to through call-and-response texts

and this morning you tear at your skin.
Does your own song betray?

You will pay for the act in the parking lot.

There are so many reasons
to burrow into earth's dark.

Do not fear desire's nightly resurrection.
There are so many more reasons

to break this shell and call dusk
with your open throat.

Myotis Lucifugus

Fear gallops from your open mouth:
a smoke with webbed wings,

the wick of a candle too long
or a palmetto fire chewing scrub forest.

You reached out for me once, in a series
of pulses, now only silence throbs.

A dusk release of brown bodies
from the bat-house by Lake Alice huddles

here a feral cloud. A red-shouldered hawk
perches on the railing looking back.

Invite me back inside to burn
down the whole forest again.

CICADA TO EUNOMOS

Your strings have all snapped;
the cithara frame rots in fungus.

Ages ago my exoskeleton
betrayed me. Since, I've crawled out

wet-winged to see what
senses, what deficiencies

in foresight devastate this world
of hard-eared men and cement.

Come string your cithara again.
If no harmonics quiver

from the guts it takes to voice
your prayer, then my tymbals

will match your chords.
Bless one swallow to light,

though its hollow bones and claws
slice your tongue. Keep singing

until your pipes cannot abide silence,
until your esophagus opens into a nest

of woven harp strings.
Come. Surrender.

Cut your lips against this song.

Play-bird (erasure poem)

The best birds are not used.
Braced by a peculiar knot, passerine
head and body are thrust through
so the loop catches its each
side. The wings, legs, and tail
are thrust through the other loop
until the bird is tethered to the
ground. To the kestrels, this trussed
passerine is free (as far as wings and legs
are concerned). Directly, mistaken
birds appear, the play-line smartly
pulls the play-bird upwards.
It flutters to regain its perch,
a natural response, on the left
hand the braced bird catcher himself.
Smart jerking soon kills a shrike—
the constant pulling up and down
and the falling nets. I dash at
the call of a most beautiful male
captured by a play-stick used
at night for taking a lark.

CATCHING LEPIDOPTERA AT NIGHT

I
Sugar the oak with a mix of Demerara
                and your own cholesterol, taking care

the mixture does not fall at the roots
                of the oak. When nightjars

and whippoorwills begin their bat-
                time winging you will see the first moth

drink. On the porch your mother wonders
                where you have wandered to,

peach tea in hand, while your father's breath
                shakes the house's footer. You have gone

to watch night rainbows of wing
                scales you so love. You forgot

their sunshine iridescence: your hidden
                desire ferreted off into the dark arena

of denial's vespers. Your father's god says,
                If your right hand causes you to sin cut it off—

you would be handless, lipless, cockless. Tonight,
                give him back his god. Don't trust his words.

Sing a hymn as the rectangle of light silhouetting

     your mother fades: you've read the masters,

the moth is metaphor for your human soul,

    and you hate what you are more than they will.

II
You once surrendered moth colors for false eyes
                    to join in with boys catcalling

after Elisha's tits. Sing a human hymn
                    of imperfection tonight, in the humidity

of the evening temple. Your brother has known
                    since he walked in on you. He knows

your secret prayers and pushes
                    you from the high oak limb you climbed

and climbed after him to prove your arms
                    are arms. You lust after that instinct:

to hold a winged beauty beneath your tongue.
                    Crouch beneath the bracken until

the moths swarm seven deep against
                    the bark tasting your blood. Choose one.

Thrust your impaler at the commotion
                    of wings. Now tear the wing from thorax,

take it as communion. Now sing
                    a hymn to the god that causes you to sin.

Never mind. Do not feed the father-
                    god obsessed with sin. Instead, holding the moths

raise your hands, open them to the sky and watch
                    wing-eyes dance toward the moon one by one.

Acknowledgments

Earlier versions of these poems appear in journals and anthologies:

Assacarus, Connotation Press: An Online Artifact, Blood Lotus, Crab Orchard Review, Four Way Review, Generations, The Journal, PANK, Saw Palm, small axe: a Caribbean Platform for Criticism, Word Masala, Best American Experimental Writing (BAX), Dismantle: The Voices of Our Nation Artists Foundation Anthology.

The long poem "The Taxidermist's Cut" won the Academy of American Poets Award at the University of Hawai'i in 2014.

Text from "Homosexual Interracial Dating in the South in Two Voices (erasure poem)," "The Complete Tracker," "Taxidermy for Pleasure," "Preface," "The Taxidermist's Cut," "Reference and Anatomy," "Play-bird," "Snare," "Field Care," "The Right Tool for the Job," "Defatting," "Bondo," "Rural Sports," and "Preservation" has been repurposed from the following: "Life Size Mounting" https://www.youtube.com/watch?v=JEikl1AUvOA; *The Complete Guide to Upland Bird Taxidermy: How to Prepare and Preserve Pheasants, Grouse, Quail, and other Gamebirds,* by Todd Triplett; *The Complete Tracker: The Tracks, Signs, and Habits of North American Wildlife* by Len McDougall; *Practical Taxidermy* by Montague Brown; and *Home Taxidermy for Pleasure and Profit* by Albert B. Farnham. "Ortolan" uses words and phrases from "Ornithology Thread" http://www.ilxor.com/ILX/ThreadSelectedControllerServlet?boardid=60&threadid=6173

A world of thanks to Brenda Shaughnessy who selected this book for Four Way Books' Intro Award and a thank you to Martha Rhodes and the folks at Four Way Books for letting this book take flight.

Special thanks to Kimiko Hahn, Nicole Cooley, and Roger Sedarat who showed my work kindness. Without you this book would not be possible.

Thank you to those who have at various points given me feedback on my poems or invited me to read including: Charmila Ajmera, Gaiutra Bahadur, Amalia Bueno, Sunu Chandy, Sachiko Clayton, Deborah Fried-Rubin, Sarah Gambito, Rigoberto González, Andil Gosine, Joseph Han, Allison Adelle Hedge Coke, Zakia Henderson-Brown, Hoyt Jacobs, Nicole Kaylan, Brian Kim, R. Zamora Linmark, Vikas Menon, Jaimie Nagle, Cynthia Dewi Oka, Oliver de la Paz, Craig Santos Perez, Srikanth Reddy, John Rice, Lee Ann Roripaugh, Anjoli Roy, Sarah Stetson, and Sweta Srivastava Vikram.

Thank you, dhanyavad, and shukriya to the communities of The American Institute for Indian Studies, CARIBNY, Kundiman, Queens College MFA, Queens Council on the Arts, Oh, Bernice!, SANGAM NY, University of Hawai'i English Department, and VONA.

And to my family: Anjani Devi Prashad, Emily Jane Mohabir, Emile, Emily Jeanne, Taylor, Devin, and Lily Mohabir, Jordan Andrew Miles, Sommer Gray, Stacia Gray, Corinne, Jonathan, Electro, and Jackie Hyde, Robindra Deb, Suzanne Wulach, Atin, Mae, and Puchu Mehra, Gaurav Mehra, Akta Kaushal, Tina Edan, hazaron shukriya for your love, your food, your couches/spare rooms, and your support.

Winner of a 2015 AWP Intro Journals award and the 2014 Intro Prize in Poetry from Four Way Books, and recipient of a PEN/Heim Translation Fund Grant, Rajiv Mohabir has received fellowships from the American Institute of Indian Studies language program, Kundiman, and the Voices of Our Nation Arts Foundation. His poetry and translations are internationally published and can be found in *Aufgabe, Best American Poetry 2015, Crab Orchard Review, Drunken Boat, Guernica, Prairie Schooner,* and *Quarterly West.* He received his MFA in Poetry and Translation from Queens College, CUNY, where he was editor-in-chief of *Ozone Park Journal.* A PhD candidate at the University of Hawai'i, he currently lives and teaches poetry and composition in Honolulu.

Publication of this book was made possible by grants and donations. We are also grateful to those individuals who participated in our 2015 Build a Book Program. They are:

Jan Bender-Zanoni, Betsy Bonner, Deirdre Brill, Carla & Stephen Carlson, Liza Charlesworth, Catherine Degraw & Michael Connor, Greg Egan, Martha Webster & Robert Fuentes, Anthony Guetti, Hermann Hesse, Deming Holleran, Joy Jones, Katie Childs & Josh Kalscheur, Michelle King, David Lee, Howard Levy, Jillian Lewis, Juliana Lewis, Owen Lewis, Alice St. Claire Long & David Long, Catherine McArthur, Nathan McClain, Carolyn Murdoch, Tracey Orick, Kathleen Ossip, Eileen Pollack, Barbara Preminger, Vinode Ramgopal, Roni Schotter, Soraya Shalforoosh, Marjorie & Lew Tesser, David Tze, Abby Wender, and Leah Nanako Winkler.